Standing Back Up Against Addiction

MELANIE ANN PERRIN

ISBN: 978-1-5356-0085-9

Standing Back Up Against Addiction is a dialogue between the author's personal life experiences as an addict and her professional life. She earned a Master's degree in Addiction Counseling and then pursued a career as an Addiction Counselor.

The book talks directly to the reader as only another addict can. With over 36 years of sobriety to her credit, the author highlights what kept, and still keeps, her sober when it seems like the disease is going to triumph over her.

To the non-addicted, this book reveals the uphill climb an addict endures in combating addiction.

There is a strong emphasis on the value of the person and encouragement to not give up on the goal of attaining sobriety. For the addict, the message is: "The disease of Addiction is something you have, but don't let it define you — it's not who you are!"

This book is dedicated to my children Dawn, Daniel, and Derek; grandchildren Devin, Chance, Daniel, Deyton, Micah, Aryah, and Cage; to every child, son, daughter, sister, brother, mom, dad, aunt, uncle, cousin, grandma, and grandpa that have suffered in life due to addiction.

A Special thanks to Kathy and Orville Johnson, Connie and Steve Smith, Candy Walker, Cindy Puetz and my Aunt Brad. Times when life was hard they supported and believed in me.

In memory of my parents who passed on to me, in their own time and circumstances when struggles occurred, to never stay down. What matters is that you stand back up, push forward, persevere, never giving up on yourself and your dreams.

Do not allow your addiction to define you. You did not ask for this disease, but you do need to learn how to manage it. Not dealing with this disease could mean devastating consequences, for some it has cost them their lives.

CONTENTS

Addicted? 1

The Face of Addiction 13

To the Addict 21

Standing Back Up 25

Reconnecting with Self................................. 33

When an addict reaches out for help, do not become blind and indifferent. Do not let what becomes for you an opportunity in allowing the addict to feel God's love and presence through you, pass you by.

MELANIE PERRIN

Addicted?

What most addicts have in common when their disease IS in control:

Hurting themselves
Self-anger and regret
Unbearable dispair
Hopelessness
Shame
Loneliness
Anxiety and fear
Loss of self-worth
Loss of self-respect
Loss of purpose
Spiritual discord
Helplessness
Turning away from all they value
Feeling unworthy
Broken
Lost
Inability to move forward
Depression
Inability to believe
Suicidal thoughts
Attempted suicides

When addiction is in control, "all you do" works against you…it's the nature of the illness to devalue self, to destroy who you are. But you can stop using and your life can become normal again. The first step is seeing that your using is a problem, recognizing that it is hurting your life, and you want to stop.

Be proud of yourself for reaching out for help.

You can do this!

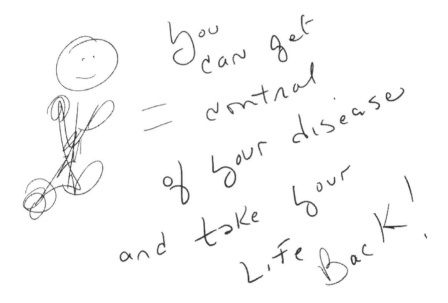

You are not your disease. Addiction is something that you have, but it isn't who you are. Do not let this disease define you. Remember the person you were before you started using, the person you know you are within. Trust that person and the life you can still have. It wouldn't be your intent to engage in behaviors that hurt you. It IS the disease, not you. You are unique and special. Always care love and value who you are, especially during the hardest of times.

When your disease is in control, it negatively impacts your life. If you're trying to stop and have been unsuccessful, don't give up. Keep trying and love yourself through it. Hold your head up. Understand that your falling back into using, even when you don't want to, is an indicator of the hold your addiction has on you. Trust yourself. You wouldn't intentionally choose to self-sabotage. I never forgot the message God spoke to me in 1979. It was to trust and have faith in him. As broken as I was, he promised with sobriety that I would get back all that my addiction had taken from me. It won't happen overnight, but it will come. It's been over 36 years, and I'm still sober, still working on me, still trusting God and he's still keeping his promise.

This Disease
does Not
deserve 1 minute....
of your time
You can break
the dependency
Stop using and
Stay Sober

The one person who should care the most about who you are is "you." For you not to care about yourself wouldn't make sense. But IT does expose your disease, left unmanaged that is where this disease takes you. It convinces you that you aren't deserving. It convinces you not to value yourself. Don't let it win. Don't settle for less. You deserve to feel good about yourself. Fight for yourself, and do not let your addiction rob you of the life you deserve.

If using drugs or alcohol would do no harm, if it would be a good thing, then there would be no reason to stop. Your life would be stable and manageable, you would be contributing to your life and others in a good way. But that isn't the case addiction hurts you, stop the destructive cycle keep reaching for recovery. Continue to stand back up against addiction, lessening its hold until you get your life back.

Say good-bye to the darkness, step into the light. Be honest with yourself about how you're using is affecting you, and how it devalues who you are. If you are tired of the devastation and pain, turn away from your addiction and say "No more!"

Trust Life as it was intended, to be Valuing who you are

Your disease keeps you in denial about how when you use, you change. That's how this disease works. It has you defending your using, even though it's negatively impacting your life. It lessens your ability to fight back by interfering with the truth. It distorts reality, which is why you need to keep challenging it. Pay attention to how you think and what you're doing with your time. Are you being the person you want to be, are you valuing yourself and the people you love?

Keep focusing on devaluing your addiction so when unexpected temptation occurs using is no longer a value. Write a list of reasons to not use then post the list somewhere in your house where you can see it every day. Make a couple copies so when you leave the house you can take a copy with you in case old using thoughts kick in you can pull your list out and read it. This interrupts your old using thoughts sometimes that is all you need to shift your thinking back to healthier thoughts that support staying sober.

Continue to focus on how your using has hurt you and what its already cost you Ask yourself, are you willing to continue to go down this destructive cycle, to continue to give alcohol or drugs all power over your life? Or can you start to push towards getting your life back by being honest with yourself around how sick you have become.

Think about this. You wouldn't give a child beer, vodka, cocaine, meth, or heroin because that would be abusive. The effects would negatively impact their reasoning so much so that they would not have control over their behaviors. They would do things they normally wouldn't do they would not be themselves. If you wouldn't do that to a child because that would be abusive, ask yourself why are you okay with doing it to yourself?

You're the one person that should always care and value who you are. Valuing yourself contributes to lessening addictions hold because this disease is fueled by not valuing self. It is not as easy as it seems because when the disease is in control its changed you to believe you are valuing yourself by using. This is the disease it's not your fault. That's why it's important to continue to focus on negative outcomes asking yourself do they revolve around your using. Keep building up that list of reasons why you want to stop using. Don't beat yourself up if you commit to sobriety only to fall back into using keep learning from it then continue with your commitment to stay sober.

Stay away from people who are using, stop taking their calls. If they stop by don't open the door. If you run into an old using friend unexpectedly don't stop to talk walk the other way.

You are already in a world where obstacles and struggles happen. But if you have this disease and your actively using obstacles and struggling continue to build.

Don't be hard on yourself if you relapse, relapse is part of the disease, use your relapse to learn from and keep standing back up against addiction towards sobriety.

Trust yourself. You wouldn't choose to be controlled by addiction, to not feel good about yourself, and to lose you're identify and life. Learn how who you are affects this disease so you can get your life back.

Love yourself through this. Keep standing back up and stepping back in line with lifestyle choices that support being the best you can be!

You deserve to experience the feeling of value, to find your purpose and be happy, and to embrace, enjoy, and feel good about "who you are." Do not let addiction take that away from you.

Take your personal power back by valuing "YOU!"

Value yourself. Be your biggest fan and advocate. When

you do that…it contributes to lessening the hold your disease has on you.

Knowledge is power. Knowledge contributes to managing your disease and lessening the hold your addiction has on you. You affect your disease every minute by how you think, how you manage your emotions, and by what you do.

If you've fallen back into your addictive behaviors, know it wouldn't have been intentional, because that wouldn't make sense or be normal for you to self-sabotage. Trust that you wouldn't intentionally choose to contribute pain to yourself or to others. But it does expose that you have this disease and the hold this disease has on you. When you're able to see that, your ability to have choice, to take your life back strengthens.

Continue to learn about who you are and why you do what you do. Do not block out the past no matter how painful. Use it to help manage your disease, and in maintaining your goals: complete sobriety, getting your life back on track, and being the person you know you are and the person your loved ones need you to be.

Faith

This disease will try to destroy your faith. Its hope is to break you down so you lose faith and shift your solution back to addiction. Don't give this disease that power. Keep faith within you. Continue to believe in the person you know you are and can be. Embrace faith especially when life gets hard. Never give up on your dreams and never stop valuing who you are!

Prayer

About prayer…I don't understand it. I obviously didn't create it, but I do know for me it works. It contributes to my disease being manageable, it lessens addictions hold. Prayer gives me strength when I have none, and helps me feel a sense of value and purpose. Prayer has always helped keep my heart in line with Gods loving and forgiving spirit. Every morning, afternoon, and end of my day I pray. Without prayer, I don't feel I would have made it. Without prayer life would be less. It's such a huge part of who I am that without prayer I'm not sure there would be me…

The Face of Addiction

Addiction isn't just a person/individual problem,
but an all-over problem…

I was watching television, and on the news the newscaster was showing a man being interviewed who had just lost his daughter in a car accident. His daughter was hit and killed by a man who was drinking and driving. The man behind the wheel never even remembered driving or the accident. However, when the man found out he had killed a young woman, he was sickened and remorseful.

The father who lost his daughter spoke out on the news. He said that the man who killed his daughter was evil, didn't deserve to live, and should be locked up in prison, never to see his family again. It was at that point that I had to turn my television off. I couldn't listen anymore because, even though I knew it was his pain talking, I was saddened.

I knew he was hurting and sending to the world the wrong message, one that hurts people, one that is toxic in keeping people sick, fueling anger and ignorance. I understood that the man was in shock and grieving, but he was using his grief to justify spreading hate, and he was playing right into addiction's hands. What killed his daughter was a man with the disease of addiction.

This was obvious to those that know and understand addiction, but for the man whose daughter was killed, using his pain to hurt himself and others, was also stepping in line with the disease that contributed to his daughter's death.

Addiction wants the world to push the addict to a place where he is unable to live with himself or get help. The man who lost his daughter locks into a mindset that keeps him and the world sick. Anger and hate interferes with his ability to grieve and heal to be in the world as his daughter needs him to be.

Addiction wants to create division and divide. Addiction wants to keep the world unhealthy that is what fuels addictions hold. Addiction knows the mindset of hate contributes pain to the world increasing tragedies that may have been prevented.

Addiction wants people to judge, hold resentments, and be angry with and feel superior to the addict. This is exactly what addiction counts on we play right into addictions hands devaluing the addict. This is a disease of shame layers of obstacles for an addict to overcome in order to get better.

In not giving an addict help, an addict's mindset is more likely to see their solution in their addiction, because an addict knows to go back to their addiction will provide them with a moment of relief and comfort, and disengage them from all their pain and spiritual bankruptcy.

When in the disease stage, instant gratification seems like the solution. The addict's ability to feel or see beyond that is impossible.

Especially when trying to reconnect with the world, an addict feels unworthy, judged and shamed by living with so many needs unmet. Having no housing, money, support, food, friends, solution, or hope pretty much removes all humanness from the addict, with nowhere to go except back to their addiction. People with addictions need to know they have somewhere to go, somewhere they can get help, feel safe, somewhere where they can strive to regain what their addiction stripped them of to feel of value and have hope. Addicts need people to recognize the person they are separate from their disease.

That is why support groups are helpful. They provide a safe place where an addict can go, where they aren't judged and shamed. This is what contributes to lessening an addiction's hold, and in baby steps allows an addict to heal. But that doesn't help with finances, employment, housing, food, and bills, trying to reconnect with everything their disease took from them seems impossible.

No one would question the man's loss and grief in the above scenario over the loss of his daughter, but do you think the man that hit and killed his daughter did it intentionally? Do you think that he woke up that day with a plan to drink and drive to kill another human being? Do you think the man made a decision that day to end his own life by choosing a life in prison, and having to live with killing another human being and hurting so many others? I don't think so. But what I do know and recognize is **the face of addiction.**

Tragedy. It's all over the history of addicted people. They do harm to themselves and to other people. That is not who they are when sober, but if an addict, that is where addiction takes you.

With addiction, who you are becomes hidden (this is where the loss of choice and the disease steps in).

It affects your reasoning, and common sense turns into nonsense or insanity. If you are questioning whether you are an addict, continue to focus on outcome, and continue to take personal inventory about your thoughts and behaviors. Do they match the person you want to be?

Outcomes expose if you are an addict and the stage your disease is in. There are short-term and long-term negative outcome indicators. Short-term indicators would be not being honest with yourself or others, choices taking you off track with who you want to be, isolating yourself from people that you are close to, getting into trouble with the law, contributing harm to yourself and the people you love, becoming lazy, and your life becoming unmanageable.

Long term you have lost all control, you become dependent on others, you have nothing to live for or believe in, your legal issues pile up and you're possible prison time, you're homeless and alone, you lost your job, family and friends, you're broke, you have spiritual disconnect and loss of hope, and you attempt suicide.

Easy to see why people would turn away from an addict. They tend to take the help you offer only to go back to their addiction, needing the same help over and over. However, that is what addiction is counting on, for the addict to hurt others, and for people to get tired of helping and walk away. The addict's inability to live with themselves, the struggle within, and the courage it takes to continue forward only another addict can understand. Addiction does not care about who you are or who it hurts.

The man who unintentionally killed the man's daughter isn't evil. Just the opposite. He is a victim of addiction. He has a disease. The addict's inability to not be able to see the crazy, the insanity in their addicted behaviors, that is the disease the hidden part that the world cannot understand.

You never know had people responded differently (prevention) to his addiction, it could have changed the course of events. If he could, don't you think he would rewind what happened? Of course he would. He has to live with himself and the fact that he took someone's life. He can never bring this life back and he can never make it right.

The one chance this man has of gaining any serenity, peace, or sense of self-value would be to give meaning to this tragedy. He can do this with the sharing of his story, how when under the influence he took a life.

The spirit of the woman who died is now a part of him and will continue to live within him. Together they could have worked as one in helping to save lives and preventing this from happening to someone else.

Putting this man behind bars allows addiction to win. Addiction wins in that it destroyed two lives, and prevention never happens.

The man with the disease of addiction could have gotten help with long-term inpatient treatment. He could have continued to heal and help other addicts through the telling of his story. Who knows how many addicts and lives could have been be saved by hearing his story (this will forever remain unclear). Instead in prison, this man faces a world of hate, judgments, resentment, and anger. This man is unable to share and educate others about…**the face of addiction.**

This man didn't ask to have this disease. It wasn't a choice. Most people do not know they have the disease until it's too late and the disease is in control.

When people are judgmental and shaming (whether they are an addict or not), they step into self-sabotage thinking. Long term this contributes to your not feeling good about yourself contributing to others negatively. Ignorance is what addiction counts on. It fuels addiction's hold and keeps America sick.

I believe what we miss at times is the miracle of prevention in helping an addict lessen addiction's hold. The tragedy doesn't take place, but the miracle is there and lives are saved.

Addicts need help. They don't need long prison terms. They are not evil, they are sick. Sick to the point of putting their lives and others at risk that isn't normal. It would never be a choice, but it does disclose and expose...**the face of addiction.**

Recognize it for what it is. That is how sick an addict gets. We have the opportunity to provide people who are that sick help with dignity and respect. This in itself is a start in helping to lessen addiction's hold.

Take the example of the man that hit and killed an innocent woman while drinking and driving. How does he stand back up in facing his community, the family that lost their daughter, his own family, his children and friends, the courts, and to live with himself when all he feels is remorse, regret, and shame? People that have the disease of addiction are sick.

Clearly, this wouldn't have been a choice anyone would have chosen for themselves, to have to live every day knowing that you took someone else's life, and then being locked up, never being able to live and engage in life yourself.

Giving meaning to this tragedy would not be to shame, judge, or label the drunk driver as a man that no longer has a face or value, but just the opposite.

Start contributing toward helping people lessen the chances of falling into addiction. Allow this man to use his story (tragedy of addiction) to keep this woman's memory alive through him in spirit, and together they can help save lives. Stop promoting hating the person and start promoting hating addiction, and help people feel respected, not shamed.

Help contribute to their feeling worthy and valued enough to get help. What you don't want to do is make life impossible for an addict to recover and continue to live. Help them to "stand back up against addiction," and get them the help they deserve. This lessens addiction's hold and creates value.

To have a good spirit is powerful, and touches many lives positively. To help an addict fight to get their life back – what a good feeling!

If you are an addict reading this book, if your life is out of control and consumed by addiction, do not give up on yourself. You have a disease. It wasn't a choice that you got this disease, but you can take your personal power back by facing your disease/addiction head-on and take the steps necessary to keep it manageable. It is possible!

One way to honor the lives taken due to addiction would be to continue forward with each day you have, giving meaning to all lives lost. If you can help an addict feel valued, especially when the addict can't give it to themselves, this helps to lessen addiction's hold. If the addict relapses, let them know your door is always open. That way the addict knows it has a safe and supportive place to go when they are ready. I have learned and trusted that it's God's timing, not mine. Unconditional love can help combat addiction's hold, and in turn, you might be saving not only their lives, but also the life of another, giving you a feeling of value and goodness.

Any unexpected suicide and death is one too many. You don't have to shame an addict. They are already consumed in shaming themselves ten thousand times more. They feel the negative consequences of their addiction every minute of every day.

Take the opportunity to not fuel addiction's hold, but to help lessen addiction's hold. In the depth of their despair, tell an addict their value.

You have the power to give an addict hope, to help them believe in themselves, and to help save a life. Do not personalize an addict's response when you reach out to help and they fall back. In fact, expect relapses, but know that reaching out has momentum and means something. It does make a difference, and will lead an addict to help sooner rather than later. Addiction is hoping that an addict is repeatedly unable to stay away from its addiction, and that the addict's family, friends, and outside support will give up on them.

Addiction wants the addict to feel alone and devalued because addiction knows that if the addict feels no hope or support, the addict will continue to get pulled back into their addiction.

The world today knows enough about addiction to know when the addicted get that sick. Start lessening addiction's hold when tragedy comes up. See it for what it is, and recognize that it's not the person, but the face of addiction.

The positive influence each one of us has to impact another is amazing. Each individual can pass hope to another, which is powerful in helping to save lives. Let's, start as a whole embracing each other with support, unconditional love, and caring especially when an addict is in despair. Judgment and selfishness is self-sabotaging to all, even the non-addicted.

To the Addict

Do not give up on yourself. You have a disease that when the disease *is* in control it impacts your life and defines you negatively. To experience over and over again the devastating consequences: loss of employment and finances, loss of family and friends, legal issues, judgment and shame, humiliation, public embarrassment, jail or prison, lost time and memories, the inability to manage your life, and the inability to move forward. Left in an unimaginable state of not knowing how to live within your own skin, feeling normal or worthy again becomes a distance dream. Your addiction seems to be your saving grace, thus keeping the destructive cycle alive.

You hear from others to believe, feeling normal, having control over your life, being responsible, feeling good about yourself will happen it just takes time. But believing and having faith gets old. Recovery seems impossible because you keep relapsing and your life continues a downward spiral. Pay attention to what's happening don't block it out learn from it, use it to increase your awareness in you're having this disease, trust it isn't who you are but it is how this disease works. The disease wants to wear you down. Don't let the disease win.

Keep standing back up by stepping back in line with lifestyle choices that support who you know you are and staying sober. Life will get better, believe in sobriety and believe in yourself. That first year can be hard but it will be worth it. You can do it. You are so much more than this disease. Stop trusting drugs or alcohol. Stop trusting what is destroying you even if it initially feels right or feels good. Those are the moments you lock your focus on past using. How it hurt you.

Allow it now to make a positive impact on your life. Never forget the pain using caused. Allow it to validate the nature of this disease, allow it to be a reminder of the natural course in how this disease works, and why today you choose not to use. Be grateful that you are not dead. Not everyone is that lucky. Be grateful that you are still alive. Fight to stay sober, to have the chance to live the life you deserve to live.

I will repeat that the hardest thing to do is to continue standing back up against addiction and stop using. Do not allow your disease to define you. Your life was not meant to be controlled by addiction you can live without addiction you need to stay sober and get through it.

It may not feel right at first because your system is conditioned to your addiction but you can recondition your system to a different behavior one that won't destroy your life. Never give up on yourself or believing that sobriety is possible. You are still alive embrace that. That is your hope. This disease is manageable, but you have to educate yourself on addiction and follow directions on how to manage it. Continue to try until, continue to fight until, continue to believe until even if you find yourself alone and no one else stands beside you. Stay strong within yourself. Know you deserve better. You did not ask for this disease, but you do need to be responsible in making healthy changes. Never give up on who you are. You deserve to live. Believe in this moment, believe in complete sobriety, believe in yourself and your future. Never underestimate your value as a person, a son or daughter, brother or sister, uncle or aunt, mom or dad, grandma or grandpa, friend or neighbor.

Do not define yourself by anyone that doesn't value you. Recognize that there might be times when it's just you and God. Be okay with that. Learn to enjoy and treasure your own company. The world is full of bad, mean-spirited people. Stay away from them.

The world is also full of loving, caring, nonjudgmental, and supportive people that will value you unconditionally. Find these people. Be around people who can accept who you are in the process of change.

Standing Back Up

View hitting bottom as an opportunity. Do not allow it to define you, but allow it to give meaning, insight, value, and purpose to your life.

It's never too late, start now. It's hard to know how to get your life back, how to go forward when your disease has you broken and shamed. To think about moving forward seems impossible. Looking at your past choices around using is painful. But you need to pick yourself back up. Believe with sobriety all things are possible! Trust your life just got better. Commit to complete sobriety embracing and feel how you're stepping in line with positive thoughts (with sobriety life will be better) and behaviors (turning away from your addiction and staying sober) create within you value. So powerful!

Commit to complete sobriety and start looking forward to your future!

As you continue forward, embrace your value to yourself and others by staying sober. No matter what else your pushing through no matter how tough your life gets keep valuing sobriety because with sobriety you have you! To use means who you are becomes blocked or hidden. Stay sober! As painful as it is to look back on your past using, it can now be used in a good way. It can help motivate you to not go back to your addiction. Keep the negative consequences of your using upfront this will help you to never want to go back. Sober, you can help others yet struggling by sharing with them your story. Staying sober passes on to fellow addicts the hope that they can recover as you have.

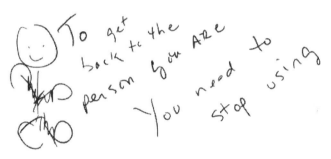

Personalize, validate, and own how your using affected you. Never forget the pain, continue to devalue your addiction so that you never turn back toward it. Keep your focus on your goal of complete sobriety, and your personal goals in affecting yourself and others positively. It's important to be with people that support your sobriety, people that understand your disease and value your courage.

Life is already hard, with this disease it becomes even harder, so it's important to build within yourself a strong mindset that values you.

Self-help meetings like Alcoholic Anonymous and

Narcotics Anonymous are wonderful resources and are free, providing sober supportive fellowship. Treatment, Individual counseling, self-help books, motivational speakers, movies, and online resources available to help you. It's hard to have hope in life when you're hurting, but that depth of pain and despair becomes your reasoning and justification in never going back, to never trust using again. Focus forward positively. Your life's about to change for the better!

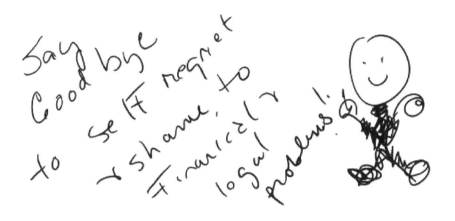

People that have never experienced addiction might not get it. All they know is when you use, you become someone that devalues yourself and others. It's hard, because you want them to understand. But it is what it is, and you have to accept it. I can honestly say that had I not been an addict, I'm not sure I would understand it. Unless you have been through it, it's hard to understand.

I'm also a cancer survivor. Had I not gone through it, I wouldn't understand what someone diagnosed and fighting cancer goes through. Because I am a survivor, it now becomes one of my values in giving support to others because I have been there. This is what your value is as well sober, giving to those still struggling and having the strength to help them push through. Focus on all you have to look forward to. When sober, you're a huge value to yourself, your family, and others.

Gravitate toward people that support you unconditionally. Relearn how to feel comfortable in your own skin. Take time and relax, read a book, watch a motivational movie, meditation and prayer whatever creates within positive energy, good spirit and supports you're staying sober. Say to yourself, "With sobriety, if that is all I have, I have hope, I have me."

You are not alone. Many people have had to rebuild their lives. You can, too. Everything you have went through contributes to who you are. The same applies to your future every minute, every blessing and set back has meaning. I have made many mistakes in my 36 years of sobriety but I feel blessed to still be alive, I have endured going backwards many times, my biggest downfall has been in trusting the wrong people this in itself brought significant tragedy and pain to my life. Cancer, poverty I could go on but I have stayed sober through it keeping my relationship with God strong. The negatives in my life have never outweighed the positives or blocked the possibilities.

It's that magical life truth that just is. If you go back to using and not value who you are, your life won't work.

What helped me reconnect with myself sober was my spending time alone in meditation and prayer.

I feel it helps strengthen my relationship with myself, and my connection with my higher power. My lifeline has always been my relationship with my higher power that I choose to call God, a God that allows my humanness to be exposed and accepted.

I believe that my higher power sees and knows who I am, and loves me through it unconditionally!

In times of struggle I seek serenity and strength, recognizing a power greater in nature. It's as simple as looking up at the sky!

Life is meant to be lived. You have one life, and one chance at embracing who you are. I believe there is a life law that says when you stay positive and do good things with your time, it normally and naturally creates within you good feelings and you experience feelings of serenity and value, AND it contributes to keeping you sober.

Paying attention to your mind/spirit, making sure it's positive important. With sobriety you control your mind.

The disease of addiction has the potential to take control and pull you back in at times when you do not pay attention to your behaviors or your thoughts. For example, if you start valuing dishonesty or spending time with using friends. Unhealthy thoughts or behaviors could lead you back to relapse. If that is the case, use your relapsing back to learn from identifying how you got pulled back in then start fresh changing back to positive behaviors and thinking, valuing yourself.

Do not give up. Keep trying, and focus in the moment. Believe in yourself 100%, put in your best effort each time, and trust you will get there! If you try, and over and over are unsuccessful despite your efforts, your efforts mean something. Remember your relapses have value.

Take time to feel bad about the relapses, validating with yourself that you aren't okay with the behavior, meaning who you are when you use, which is a good thing because if you were okay, you wouldn't want to quit.

Feel the pain. Process through it normally. Use it now to learn from, and then self-forgive and continue forward with your commitment to staying sober. Find friends that are supportive, caring and nonjudgmental, attend self-help meetings you don't have to do this alone!

Do not beat yourself up. Keep striving to reach your goal in getting your disease managed. Remember, this disease hurts when it's in control. You need to keep standing back up with dignity and respect. Fight to live, and fight to get your life back.

Believe that you have a higher power that knows and sees your suffering, and that knows the person you are separate from your addiction. Believe your higher power is helping you. Trust in the person you know you can be. Trust in a power that is greater than you, who loves and cares for you. Share with your higher power your pain and your desire to be sober. With sobriety you have you. Be good with that and the rest will come. Commit yourself to living differently, stepping in line with thoughts and behaviors that value you. What is the worst that can happen?

Reconnecting with Self

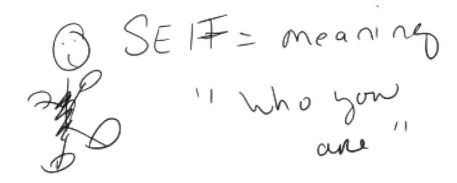

The disease of addiction takes you away from who you are. You have to relearn how to live sober. You do this by reconnecting with self.

Self = who am I? Finding you're way back to who you are takes time, start by keeping it simple. Valuing who you are by staying sober.

Reconnect with self through stepping back in line with your role-expectations. Your first role-expectation is to value you!

Makes sense doesn't it? In life, the one person who should

care the most about "who you are" is you. To not value self
(who you are) just wouldn't make sense.

Value self = complete sobriety.

Then step back in line with your other role-expectations.
For example: if being a parent is one of your roles then the
expectation would be for you to be the adult they need and
depend on you to be. When you use, addiction takes you away
from your role expectations.

Stepping back in line with your role-expectations creates
value and you feel good about who you are. Lessening
addictions hold.

You also reconnect with self by reconnecting with your
feelings. You're thinking contributes to how you feel. Changing
your thoughts to positive thoughts, thoughts that don't do
harm to self and/or others. Thoughts that will normally and
naturally create good feelings and value within self-lesson's
addiction hold.

Let me show you what I mean through example.
Look at the first example.

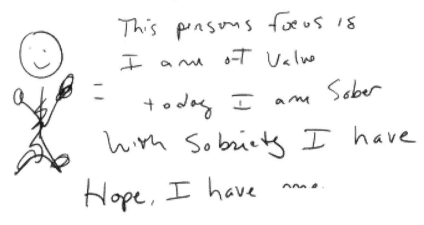

Look at this next example.

Which of the above examples is the happier person? If you picked the first example, you are right. Look at how your thoughts contribute to how you feel. The second scenario would make anyone depressed, and for an addict this type of negative thinking is exactly what can trigger a relapse. Negative thinking creates you to feel bad. When you feel bad, it can contribute to your choosing to use because you want to change how you feel. Feeling bad is hard to tolerate, so you want to feel good again. It's so easy to get pulled back in.

That is why learning how this disease works, and how it uses you, to self-sabotage is vital so you can make the changes needed to successfully manage your disease and maintain complete sobriety.

Learn about your disease and how to manage it. You deserve to get your life back and enjoy your life!

One thing you can't do is run away from self, meaning who you are. You have to live with yourself every day. Your thoughts and your behaviors always have consequences. They are either good or bad. They impact you either positively or negatively.

Though, a lot of things can block you off from self like addictions, dysfunction or abuse. But who you are, how you think and what you do with your time there is always a consequence.

How you think and your actions contributes to how you affect your disease. When you think positively, have a good spirit and do good things with your time = it automatically, normally and naturally creates with in you value and good feelings. If you feel good because of who you are and what you're doing your less apt to go back to using because you're not willing to feel the pain that comes with it.

Since addiction contributes to devaluing self when you value self it contributes to lessoning addictions hold. The more you step in line with things that create value normally and naturally your reasons to use lessens/stops.

Keeping focusing on wanting to feel of value, feeling good about yourself sober engaging in healthy thoughts and activities leaving behind the negative consequences caused by using. Say to your addiction no more!

If you're still using ask yourself this question: Are you continuing to go toward behaviors, attitudes, beliefs, and values that continue to cause and create pain in your life?

If your answer is yes think about what needs to change,

it starts with you. Start trusting the behaviors that aren't self-sabotaging that will value you and the people you love. When you can do that, you know you are on the right path in managing your disease.

I can't say enough about the importance in paying attention to how you think. Your mind is the one thing sober you can control. But if you are an addict and actively using you lose the ability to control your mind. Slowly the disease takes control. If you're still using, get the help you deserve. Stop using and take your life back.

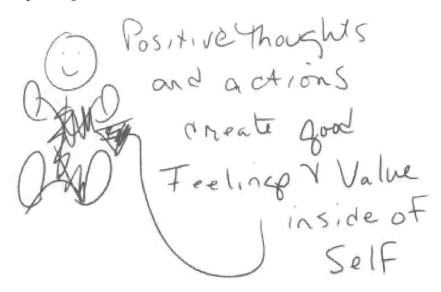

What contributes to staying sober is doing good things in life that contribute positively to yourself and/or others, it automatically creates value and good feelings inside of self.

This contributes to lessening addiction's hold, connects you with self, builds positive self-esteem, and makes you like and feel good about who you are. People come toward you and they enjoy being around you.

When you engage in thoughts or behaviors in life that create harm to self or others, it automatically lessens value, and creates bad feelings inside yourself.

Negative thoughts or creating harm to others contributes to fueling addiction's hold because it normally and naturally creates within feelings that don't feel good. Don't allow addiction to pull you in anymore!

Keep standing back up even when you make mistakes. You're human. It's going to happen. Continue to learn how to manage your emotions genuinely and be honest. And continue toward being the person you know you are. Do not give up on yourself. Be kind to yourself and be positive. Believe in yourself, and find people that support and love you. If you have relapsed, use the relapse as an opportunity to give meaning to your life. Then, step back in line and focus on this moment of sobriety. Empowerment comes from embracing, valuing, and caring about who you are, and trusting that you wouldn't have intentionally relapsed or taken a step back. It could identify an area you need to change, or past issues that need to be resolve.

It's time to rebuild your life. Create good energy and a positive spirit. Look forward to the challenge, as tough as it is, and know that you can do this. If you feel you have hit bottom, that's okay. You know where you are if you're at the bottom. That means you have to build up! Stay in gratitude and feel blessed for this opportunity. This is your time to grow and reconnect with self and the world. This is an opportunity to pay attention to who is around you, and who reaches out to you to help you to stay sober and rebuild. Those are the people you want in your life.

I don't think anyone can fully understand how you lose choice with this disease, how you can continue to self-sabotage and not get it. No one knows the depths of despair and darkness of addiction unless you've been there. That is where the value comes into play, when one addict shares his story with another. But it doesn't mean that others don't love you and don't care, because they do. They might need time for you to stay sober before coming back around. That's okay. You need to trust that.

Start trusting what has worked for others follow their direction. You are a huge value. Keep standing back up against addiction and you will make it. :)

When living a foot in and a foot out, and still consumed by addiction. When you feel the addiction within you, but you're not ready yet to let go?

Sounds pretty stupid. Why would anyone want to hang on to an addiction if they can see that addiction has a hold on them?

To the addict this makes sense. They know their life would be better if they could just leave their addiction in your past. But it's like a wild monster when it comes alive inside. All in you lights up and is on fire. It is that strong. To go against that seems not only impossible, but also wrong. It feels so right in the moment even though you know it's wrong.

If you go back into your addiction, forgive yourself. Keep standing back up and refocusing on your goals, and step back in line with thoughts and behaviors that normally and naturally create value (role-expectations). Continue to devalue your addiction by remembering the pain and shame your addiction costs you. It's when you minimize and forget the pain that it contributes toward going back. Keep the pain up front. Keep up front a mindset that devalues your relationship with your addiction.

Be strong in your faith. Tap into what's within you. If your open to it engage in daily meditation and prayer. Change your beliefs to ones that support valuing yourself and sobriety. Find friends that support you unconditionally. Stay focused. Continue to ask yourself if your thoughts and behaviors match the outcome you want. Live in the moment and embrace the present. You are of value. Believe in yourself and know that you can have a good, happy life. Be patient and trust time. It's on your side! Believe that even in the darkest of times, you are of value. Even if you fall back into addiction, stand back up, step back in line with things that create within you value and good feelings, and stay focused on the good. Feel good that at this time you are sober. Use your relapse as a tool to learn from and view it now as a value to help others who have relapsed and in need of a supportive person to talk to. Learn from your history, forgive yourself, and focus forward positively.

God is good, and God is always around you, loving you and wanting you to value who you are every day, to live a good life, and to be happy. Imagine the times when you feel you've fallen short, and God's hand reaches out to help you back up. God loves you unconditionally. He knows your pain and past journey. I believe he is my biggest advocate and friend always with me.

If you are feeling down, hurt, and helpless, trust and know that you are not alone. Share your pain with God. It cleanses and re-energizes your spirit, and then let go and let God. God is always available and will help you stand back up.

Your history is past information that you can continue to look back over and learn from in so many ways. The value that your personal history holds is huge, but I understand no one wants to relive past pain.

Sounds easier to decide to just live in the moment and continue forward positively. It sounds less painful and simpler. However, what happens if you do that without looking back and learning from your history? You miss out on the opportunity to allow your past to carry meaning forward, especially for an addict. It is very dangerous territory when you minimize or choose to block out or process through unresolved past issues. You become vulnerable and risk falling back into addiction and dysfunction. Addiction hopes you don't resolve past issues.

It is very important to find a good addiction counselor to process your history. With so many important areas and stages, especially in your childhood, you might miss something unintentionally. When it's just you looking back, you wouldn't think that certain areas are important to process, discuss, and learn from. That is where the skill of a good clinician comes into play.

Recovery is about stepping back in line with things that create within you normally and naturally good feelings and value. I have always felt there is a life rule: Good is good and bad is bad.

You can lessen addiction's hold by stepping back in line with what is good, valuing your role-expectations first step by valuing you by paying attention to how you think and what you do with your time. Then by valuing your other roles. If you are a parent, value your children. If you are a husband, value your wife. When you step away from your role expectations, that fuels addiction's hold because you won't feel good about yourself. But when you step back in line with your role expectations, you lessen addiction's hold and feel good about yourself.

Addictions take you away from your heart, from who you are, and who you love. Your heart is your ticket to living. As it beats within, pay attention.

Do not let addiction disconnect you from the things that matter the most. You are the one that has to fight to take your life back. Recognize…**the face of addiction.** Do not let it win.

Do not live your life following in someone else's path. Follow your own uniqueness and passions. But it's important that it's something positive that will contribute to your life and the ones you love in a good way. This will become clearer over time if it isn't apparent yet. Stay sober and overtime you will know what your purpose and value in life is supposed to be.

Keep it simple, start by stepping back in line with role expectations, valuing self and family.

Find something that you can look forward to doing, something that brings excitement into your life. There is only one you, and it's important that you do what is important to you, with personal responsibility of course. :)

This is your power in combating addiction.

Addiction does not personalize. However, everything about addiction is personal. When you continue to engage in behaviors that take you away from the person you want to be, then those behaviors are a problem.

If you have the disease of addiction, this is how the disease works. It takes you away from who you are. Addiction doesn't personalize the pain it causes you but every way you are affected by this disease is personal.

No one plans on being an addict, but it happens to the best people, the nicest people, and to the very good compassionate, caring, and loving people. Addiction is slick. It knows you inside and out, and if an opening arises, it has no mercy.

What we do know is addiction is a horrible disease that lives within the addict, and if it is given the chance, it will destroy you.

You are not alone. Many people have this disease. Identify how this disease is hurting you, how it's impacted your life. Pay attention and focus on how your mind works and what you're doing with your time that leads you towards using. Then do the opposite. Step in line with behaviors and thoughts that create within you good feelings and value. Stop using is not that simple so get help. You are deserving of help do not feel shame.

Addiction takes you away from the things that would normally allow you to experience self-worth and self-respect. Identity and recognize this, in order to motivate change. When pulled under by addiction, addiction takes away your choice.

That is the devastation of this disease, and instead of being happy and living a life of purpose, the addict experiences loss of self and purpose living becomes hard for some death becomes the solution.

Think about it. Who in their right mind would want to be an addict? I don't believe anyone would choose to lose choice, but that is where addiction takes you. That is how addiction is recognized and identified, because we already know that no one healthy would choose to go there if given a choice. The addict deserves to get help to get back to being themselves and not allow addiction to destroy who they are. Remember the long list of outcomes listed on the first page when the disease of addiction is in control? Think about this. Why would anyone intentionally continue to go toward behaviors or attitudes that contribute so much pain in their lives? I don't think anyone would, but it does expose **the face of addiction.**

Talking to a recovering addict helps. Reach out to them as they can understand you as no one can. They understand the remorse and pain you are feeling, because they have been there. They can also relate to the devastation you feel each time your addiction takes hold, only to leave you less than what you were before. They understand the genuineness of your words as you swear to never go toward your addiction again, only to be pulled back under again and again. When or if this has happened to you, do not beat yourself up and do not give up on yourself. That would be playing right into addiction's hands, and that is exactly what addiction counts on you doing. When you give up on yourself, or are too hard on yourself, it fuels addiction's hold. You give life to it, contributing toward your self-destruction. Instead, believe in yourself and know that it wasn't your intent to relapse back into your addiction.

Feel good that you aren't okay with who you are when you

fall back into your addiction, because that isn't the person you want to be. That is your strength, and that is your hope. Trust and know that that is your personal power in fighting back, lessening addiction's hold.

Give meaning to each relapse and continue forward, recognizing it isn't who you are but it is ...**the face of addiction.**

Keep fighting to be the person you know you are.

Focus on intent. This helps you to see yourself for who you are, separate from your disease it helps you to heal and to forgive yourself. Trust your intent. It wasn't your intent to sabotage yourself. If it was, that wouldn't make sense, because the one person that should always care about you "is you."

Keep loving and caring about yourself, keep having the faith and trust that you will get past it, and learn from your history, especially your relapses. No matter how painful, allow it to give meaning to this moment, and then continue forward, trusting yourself. Continue to be there for yourself. Addiction consumes and cripples you. Know and trust that it isn't part of who you are but accepting it is the disease. Continue to believe in who you are, and know you are of value. Do not shame yourself or others who are struggling with addiction. As you know, it wouldn't be a place anyone would choose to be. "There is hope" and "there is you." Know that you are not alone. Continue to take a stand. Love, care, and support yourself, and continue to combat addiction by valuing "who you are" by valuing you every day.

The hardest thing to ask of an addict is to say good-bye to their relationship with their addiction. That doesn't make sense due to the pain that addiction causes, but for an addict it can be true.

It's hard to imagine recovery, and hard to image feeling good about yourself as you lost so much of your spirit and soul, not being the person you want to be or the person who you know you are. Do not allow addiction to take that from you anymore. Know that you deserve better. You deserve your life back. You deserve to be you. Image yourself happy and whole again.

Keep pushing forward and focus on doing things with your life that create value being the person you want to be and say good-bye to your addiction today. Be your biggest fan, your biggest advocate and best friend.

Keep pushing forward, don't give up, continue to persevere combating your addiction. As you make changes your brain is changing. With changes taking place your brain is also having to adjust. This might take some consistent reinforcement at first because your brain might resist. There may be times your mind will want to bounce back into its old way of thinking it is your job to catch it and stop it, redirecting it back to your new way of thinking that supports valuing you and sobriety. Addiction leads you away from who you are and what you value. Addiction wants you back, and it doesn't give up easily. It wants you to devalue, your values. How powerful is that! Fight back by stepping back in line with the behaviors and thoughts that create value within yourself getting back to the person you know you are and deserve to be.

Know you are of value no matter how badly you feel right now. Do not give up on yourself.

Addiction is "Slick" — it gives off the illusion that it is throwing you a lifeline. No one book could cover all its tricks because each individual deals with issues unique to who they are and gets pulled under differently. No one can see entirely someone else's issues (what's behind the eyes), but what we can do is give out good information, and then add a good addiction counselor that will go over your life to help you to work through past/current unresolved issues. That would be the icing on the cake in creating the armor against addiction. Do not give up on the person you deserve to be. You deserve to experience joy, love, respect, and happiness!

Addiction does not have the right to interfere with a person's soul and destiny. Choose every day to create a foundation that "values self" and that "values who you are!"

By valuing self, you start to combat and lessen the chance of falling into addiction's hold.

Start by creating a new foundation, one that validates you!

Addiction works from the inside out. Addiction takes over insofar as it changes who you are and you don't even see it coming. It slowly gets you to lower your personal standards. It is detected by how you think, changes in attitudes and beliefs that lead you into self-destructive behaviors and away from family.

It is inconceivable how any addict has the ability to find the courage to fight back when all around them and within, they feel judgment and shame. If you are an addict still struggling do not allow your disease to define you. It's not who you are. Recognize your addiction is killing you and get help. You are better and more than your addiction. Addiction does not deserve one second of your time.

YOU ARE HERE BECAUSE GOD INTENDED FOR YOU TO BE. YOU ARE OF VALUE. YOU DESERVE TO ENJOY WHO YOU ARE AND TO BE HAPPY. KNOW THAT GOD LOVES YOU UNCONDITIONALLY. GOD IS HERE TO HELP YOU. AS HIS CHILD GOD WANTS YOU TO COME TO HIM HE UNDERSTANDS AND WILL NEVER JUDGE OR SHAME YOU. YOU ARE IMPORTANT, SPECIAL, UNIQUE, AND DESERVING IN EXPERIENCING BEING THE PERSON YOU WERE MEANT TO BE!

I experimented with alcohol for the first time when I was fourteen. The effects of alcohol felt empowering. I would say it was my decision to continue to use however overtime unforeseen to me the choice to use was no longer an option. My drinking increased from abuse to dependence in a very short time. I could not see beyond my need to drink the pull unimaginably inhumane. Addiction took me down fast. When I wasn't capable of lifting a glass, I was passed out. I don't have full memories — I only have slight recalls in between blackouts. The person I became under the influence unrecognizable, the person I was unreachable. My inability  to develop and experience life as life was intended lost, relationships and memories ended. Addiction could have taken my life easily. I know I am lucky to be alive. By the grace of God, I haven't had a drink since August 1979. I was very sick, hallucinating, suicidal, high anxiety and fearful. I sobered up cold turkey which I would not recommend anyone do. I trusted God's guidance. He was my lifeline. As broken and as damaged as I was when others gave up on me God never did. I trusted God hadn't forgotten the person I was before my addiction and I believed if I stayed sober God would help me get back to being the person I was. God gave me his strength never allowing me to give up on myself. God's presence has gotten me through the hardest and loneliness of times. I will never know why God chose to save me, but I have always felt that it had less to do with me, and more to do with my children. It is also his will in my writing this book, passing on to others what he has passed on to me.